Second Life:

Poems of Re-emerging

Other books from Redhawk Publications:

All I Wanted by Jake Young

Birdhouse by Clayton Joe Young and Tim Peeler

The Bost-Burrus House by G. Leroy Lail and Richard Eller

Bouquets Hadn't Been Invented Yet by Tony Deal

Food Culture Recipes from the Henry River Mill Village

From Darkness: The Fated Soules Series, Book One by Jan Lindie

Going To Wings by Sandra Worsham

The Hickory Furniture Mart: A Landmark History by G. Leroy Lail and Richard Eller

Hickory: Then & Now by Richard Eller and Tammy Panther

Hickory: Then & Now The Complete Texts by Richard Eller

Hickory: Then & Now The Complete Photograph Collection

Hurdles by Ric Vandett

The Legends of Harper House – The Shuler Era by Richard Eller

More by Shelby Stephenson

Mother Lover Child & Me by Erin Anthony

Newton: Then & Now by Richard Eller and Sylvia Kidd Ray

Piedmont The Jazz Rat Of Cunningham Park by Mike Bruner

A Place Where Trees had Names by Les Brown

Polio, Pitchforks & Perseverance by Richard Eller

Sanctuary Art Journal 2018, 2019, 2020

Secrets I'm Dying to Tell You by Terry Barr

Sittin' In with the Sun by Carter Monroe

Sky Full of Stars and Dreams by Scott Owens

Sleeping Through the Graveyard Shift by Al Maginnes

Suffragettes by Harriett Bannon and Brigette Hadley

Waffle House Blues by Carter Monroe

We Might As Well Eat by Terry Barr

We See What We Want to See: The Henry River Mill Village in Poetry, Photography, and History by Clayton Joe Young and Tim Peeler

What Came to Me—Collected Columns Vol One by Arlene Neal

Win/Win by G. Leroy Lail

Second Life:

Poems of Re-emerging

Kyra Freeman

REDHAWK
PUBLICATIONS

Published By REDHAWK PUBLICATIONS

2550 US Hwy 70 SE

Hickory NC 28602

Robert Canipe, Publisher and Editor-in-Chief
Tim Peeler, Editor
Patty Thompson, Project and Permissions Coordinator
Author photo by Kristy Bright
Flame photograph on page 38 by Mel Freeman

ISBN: 978-1-952485-24-4

Table of Contents

Acknowledgements

My gratitude goes out to Angela Shores at Adventure Bound Books for her work in supporting writers in the Morganton area. Thank you to Redhawk Publications for offering this opportunity for me to publish this chapbook as part of the Adventure Bound Books and City of Morganton Celebrating Poetry Contest. Thank you to the Wildebeests Poetry Peeps: Deb, Patty, and Becca, for all their encouragement in person and via Zoom. I would like to thank my family for their support of my creative endeavors. Thanks goes out to Olly for lending me her sense of artistic flow for this book; to Eva and Priya for just being there and for listening to my poems even when they are cringe-worthy; to my sister, Daria, for riding with me in the manure spreader of life; to my father, David, who drove; to my mother, Donna, for years of telephone support; to Shirley for raising a son with a sense of humor as big as his sense of adventure; and to my husband, Mel, for his facility with metaphor and unconditional love.

Poetry's Music by Shelby Stephenson

Kyra Freeman's *Second Life: Poems of Re-emerging* reads as if eye-lids open every morn, as bones begin to creak – rise. The sun remembers. Provinces adorn neighborhoods. Children hold hands. Dogs bounce tennis balls. Furniture awakens to doggy's wagging tail – "Outside! Outside!"

Magic rules, as a "second life" dances with a partner, baggage and all, back to the first of things when Time somehow started and words began to work the way they do. A meadow, by another name could be metaphor for a kitten to play with a moth that misses a flame in a daydream as one wonders if a house pet wants to be let out – to be, to see, to let something "personal" lead to syllables spoken with necessity. Self-portraits grow from one and two until the past grows thorns, shackles – until "Kicking my ankles loose, I walked forward in a straight line towards the sun."

April rebels, "raining when it wants to."

The poet looks around in "vibrations of rebirth."

-- Shelby Stephenson was poet laureate of North Carolina, 2015-2018. His recent books: *More* (Redhawk Publications) and *Shelby's Lady: The Hog Poems* (Fernwood Press).

Shady Rest

Black snake climbs the trunk,
Safe between ground and sky, she
Lets the shed skin fall.

Happily Banished

The sounds of wind chimes,

And the whirligig,

And my daughters playing at the playground down the road

Float.

I can almost see them from the front porch,

To where I am

Happily banished.

"Sisters only!"

(The dog doesn't count.)

The evening cool begins to settle as the birds sing the sun lower in the sky.

The ease of this moment, so hard-won,

Is priceless.

The Warmth of Neighborhood

On our front porch

I pause to breathe in the warmth of neighborhood.

The Sunday solo of redemption soars from the parking lot as

A little sister holds ribbons while a big sister brushes,

Releasing stray strands of long black hair to the birds.

A football lobbed into six-year-old hands wobbles and bounces around the corner.

That wooden fence I had erected does not obscure the tang of lit charcoal

Or the memory of the neighbor grilling shirtless.

A cat steals outside to lie in wait under parked cars and

My muzzle-blackened dog digs out a flowerbed tennis ball.

The cruiser asleep on a lawn signals that the policeman is off today.

A mother and grown daughters in pink and purple sneakers

Chase each other for another lap around the block as

Lace curtains part across the street.

Pollen-speckled water from a lovingly washed truck winds snake-like into our yard.

The warm breeze tags along as the groceries and I head inside.

Sometimes the days of ease give way,

The door is closed against the claws of fear, and

The porch stands empty.

Darkness descends and transforms into those nights

When my purse is stolen from my unlocked car,

When an unknown van slowing by our house makes my husband's heart race,

When the ambulance flashers' sudden reflection is magnified in black windows,

When a helicopter and a gunshot echo inside the city limits,

When we do not feel safe enough to shake hands.

Those nights will give rise to morning

And bring walking dogs,

And Wednesday trash cans on the curb,

And Eugene's mail truck squeaking as it rounds the corner.

We neighbors will wave and stop to chat and reintroduce ourselves.

Someone will mount the steps to leave a gift

On our front porch.

Buried Treasure

Beyond the coffee maker,

Daylight drips onto the kitchen floor.

The window over the sink is a neon sign flashing: "Outside! Outside!"

"Come!"

The dog's tail lifts

As he rubs the sleep from his eyes

And shakes his aging joints.

"Let's go out."

"We'll look for treasures."

He knows that the little slip of woods behind our house

Holds magic.

I get on my boots and bring my coffee cup.

The noise of truck brakes slowing down for the light at the end of Enola Road

Punctuates the birdsong.

The neighbor's dog barks from his pen.

And we are out, crossing our one-third of an acre

To the back owned by the woods.

What will we find this morning?

I watch for snakes and wild spring flowers with every spongy stride.

There was once a twisted unicycle

Buried under decaying leaves.

A branch emerging from the bank that I had almost cut down

Now erupts in pink flowers.

The neighbors' daffodil ignored the fence

And snuck into our yard through the trees.

Water left over from last night's rain

Exposes arteries of red dirt in the brilliant green of moss.

The dog finds a neat pile of deer droppings,

Then a stick, the perfect size for his mouth.

He parades it in triumph back to me.

A mosaic of old mirror shards lines the bed of the ditch behind the building.

I bend to pick up a piece of glass and cool rust-mud stains my hands.

The dog and I are painted in stripes of sun and shadow as

We inhale the smell of the trees reclaiming their rightful territory.

These woods have unearthed another treasure

Covered by the muck of adulthood.

I remember, yes!

I used to climb trees like ship rigging

And gather milkweed and acorn caps as an offering to the fairies

Out behind the compost pile in the one corner of my yard where my father never mowed.

I had forgotten what some part of me still seeks:

My playground.

Second Life

Veil off, eyes open,

I chose this partner.

I choose this dance.

Love is more powerful than fear.

With all of his brilliance,

      His impulsiveness,

      His baggage,

      His insight,

      His fallibility,

      His courage,

      His humanness,

      His facility with metaphor,

      His insistence on the truth,

I chose this partner.

When I can't see,

When he won't see,

When he can't talk,

When he won't let me try to help,

The pattern spirals on repeat.

Our ghosts dance with each other,

Twisting, writhing, tethered.

They drag our living selves

Over the shards of the past

Which try to embed themselves into

Our naked feet.

My feet, having shed my boots,

Those beautiful, expensive, ill-fitting boots

With a lifetime warranty

That seemed like they should have been all the rage in Paris,

Over the years I got so used to limping that

It became a part of my personal choreography;

My feet ache to learn a new dance.

My feet, having shed not only my boots but also my old skin,

Feel those shards press painfully into the newly exposed soles.

Step, step, step, sway.

We dance, moving again to our own tune, the rhythm of right now.

Our hands reach for each other and hold tight.

Veil off, eyes open,

I chose this dance.

I choose this partner.

Love is more powerful than fear.

Eight-Pound Anchor

My eight-pound anchor careens off windowsills and

Skids across the wooden floors,

Her tail expanded

Over a leftover piece of string.

The leaf brought in by the dog's tail

Sends her pouncing straight up,

Spring-toed.

She reminds me to pay attention to this moment and to laugh.

She snoozes in inconvenient places.

Purring on my foot, she reminds me to

Add softness to my breathing

And moor myself to the here and now.

An Abundance of Love: or I Should Really Call My Mother Back…

Purchasing coffee in bulk, having 160 servings

Delivered to the house at a time,

I notice, cup by cup, as it is consumed down to almost nothing.

I can never buy enough, it seems.

Who drinks all that fancy coffee, the

Kind that I special-order for my husband and me?

The children? My mother-in-law, who I know prefers a cheaper brand?

Is someone just making it, rejecting it, and then throwing it away?

Oh the dishes in the sink tell a tale!

I re-order.

I can never buy enough, it seems.

The more coffee I drink,

Having given up sugar so the flavor really matters more now,

The more coffee I drink,

The faster my mind-wings beat,

A moth drawn to the flame of scarcity,

Consumed, all-consuming

I can never be enough, it seems.

What is the opposite of scarcity?

What do I have in my life that cannot be consumed,

That cannot be taken out from under me,

Unexpectedly, unpredictably,

In this time of uncertainty,

In this house crowded with family, all waiting for the end or some new beginning,

What do I have?

I have...

I have...

I have...

An abundance of love.

Brewed, sipped, savored,

Cup after cup, it is an endless pot.

Houseperson Escapes

My beloved windowsill calicat

    chirps and clicks at the birds.

Safe here in the big warm house

    she taunts the hawk on the powerline.

I wonder if she knows that there are foxes in the woods and a herd of stray cats living

    in the burned-out house down the road.

And that the tree she longs to climb shelters a snake five times the size of her tail.

She skulks under the couch to wait by the edge of the front door

    for that moment when the wind catches it before it can close all the way,

Or when we come in, arms so full of delivered supplies that we cannot see our own feet.

A dart of cat flies by, heart racing with the thrill of exchanging safety for freedom,

    and lands hunkered under the car.

The house cat has escaped

    ...or maybe I let her out.

Belly, Claws, Teeth

Grown bored with pens and plastic mice
We turn to larger prey.
We know that simple, age-old trap
Will work again today.

Soft white feline belly bait
Come stroke my underneath!
Fool humans are so easy,
so sure in their belief

That purring means we love them,
As killer claws we sheath.
The flick of the tail is all it takes,
False sign we come in peace.

Come closer, silly human
Feel belly, claws, and teeth!
Ha! Got you again!
So what, we broke the rhyme.
Human rules do not apply.

Wisdom of the Father

I just got off the phone with my father.

After the years of awkwardly forced conversations with me

       clinging to his attention, seeking his approval,

This time was pleasantly easy.

I called him. He answered.

We walked around with our phones,

       passing into our respective kitchens a thousand miles apart.

We worked on our individual kitchen projects while talking of death and life.

We laughed with the same dark sense of humor.

He talked of his legal and financial preparations for his death,

       how he did not want to be a complication.

He talked of his schemes, his research,

       his kitchen and garden chemistry experiments

       to keep death at bay for as long as possible.

I talked about my work of seeking healing, with no paycheck but hope.

We talked of chemistry,

The interconnected evolution of plant and viruses,

The wisdom of the old ones, the ancients.

We talked of insurance, investments, the inheritance

       of a predisposition to worry about tomorrow.

We did not speak of cancer.

We did not need to speak

       of love.

Self Portrait 2

Everflowing, rushing, moving and changing,

Forceful, full of energy, and teeming with life,

The river is always here.

Sometimes the green stone and silver-fish shine through glass-clear waters,

See how the shadow of the floating leaf falls,

Hear the whisper, reach out and feel her cool softness.

The river is always here.

Sometimes mirrored, all she shows to the world is the world above,

Sometimes obscured in fog, invisible even to herself,

The river is always here.

Sometimes filled with the debris of storms,

Bruised, swollen, silt-choked, churning, smelling of sewage,

Her banks move around obstacles, pushing blindly against all that is in the way.

The river is always here.

Sometimes a dam sends her waters through turbines,

Stealing power and taking her vibrancy for the entertainment of others.

In time, she wears down the concrete,

Carving a path through immobile rocks to find new banks.

The river is always here.

Waters rise to the air and return, cycling endlessly,

Healing herself and nurturing verdant life.

The river is always here, always here, always here, flowing.

Past Life Regression

Last week, the past reached out June-green tendrils and grabbed my ankles.

The past has thorns.

It has breath that smells of wild raspberries not quite ripe.

It spoke with a soothing scratchiness.

> "Dear Rabbit," it whispered inside my head.
>
> "Remember, there is safety in numbers.
>
> Not so long ago, you made your life in this thicket.
>
> The brambles are still here, here for your protection. It is a cozy thicket.
>
> I will feed you my berries and leaves like I always used to.
>
> The twitchy-nosed zig-zaggers, the brown soft ones are so quiet, just like you.
>
> There is no need to worry so much about foxes,
>
> They only kill a few, here and there.
>
> Weasels and stray dogs hardly matter. No cause to let your heart race.
>
> Come, live here in the shade with the other rabbits!
>
> Remember, there is safety in numbers."

I shook my head clear from the green-brown illusion of safety.

> "Nnno," I whispered in reply.
>
> "The thicket is not my home. I will no longer live as prey!"

Kicking my ankles loose, I walked forward in a straight line towards the sun.

Terrible Beauty

Should I edit out the dark?

The red cardinal flies, soaring with my heart, coming so close to where I stand that I can see its beak.
Should I forget the part where the bird smashes into the window, breaking its neck and
Leaving a smear of blood to clean?

There is so much suffering in the world it is a wonder that it stays in orbit.
And yet there is also so much beauty.

Right Now

Right now donuts are hot and dripping with glaze as warm as my waiting tongue.

Right now the sun streams through the window as the napping cat basks in its spotlight, her warm calico purrs a siren of slumber.

Right now our teenagers are singing in the kitchen while cooking ever more pasta with butter and cheese.

Right now the trees in the yard are dancing in the wind and the world smells of fresh-cut grass.

Right now my fingers are stained with tie-dye colors purple, pink, and blue.

I do not know what the world will bring.

Right now, right now is everything.

April's Rebellion

And April breaks all the rules...

Planting hope and

Raining when it wants to.

Insistent, it pushes flowers through sidewalk cracks and

Lightness through my closed fingers.

Deep in the Quiet of December

Deep in the quiet of morning, before

Even the dog is awake

Chill wraps its arms around my shoulders and

Embers slowly catch the edge of the sky.

Momentum eases.

Branches play slow wind music.

Enfolded by the peace of the sleeping household the

Remaking of the world begins.

Hello and Goodbye, Mr. Dave

How do I say goodbye when you never really said hello?

I can count the conversations I have had with you in forty-five years

On one hand. And yet, I remember your hands being so much a part of my life.

The little girl me, maybe four, remembers the barn full of groceries

And the orange summer daylilies of your sister's in Cornwall.

My parents picked up supplies to feed us as I stayed out of the way.

I remember you, your long brown hair moving in the summer breeze,

No, your own constant movements rippling out to your hippie's hair,

Sun glinting from your glasses, you talked earnestly about saving the world from doom.

Your hands gestured to the ground, air, and mountains while handing us our food.

I remember my mom working at the bike and ski center. She who could neither bike nor ski.

The piles of paper were deep as the stairs to the office were steep.

The creaking old wooden floors were flecked with bike grease and the ski wax.

The smell of bike tires mixed with the click, click, click when I turned the pedals.

Your hands adjusted the training wheels for me, helped with the brakes.

I still use the skis we bought from you decades ago and think of you every time.

That parade when you rode the bicycle from 100 years ago with the giant front tire,

The playing card bicycle, I thought you were the coolest dude ever.

You mounted that enormous thing with such grace. In my memory, you were even dressed for the part.

I remember you as my father's friend. You rivaled him in grouchiness.

You both loved machines of any kind, and the two of you would talk about them

The way my mother talked to her friends about people and babies.

The motorcycle with the sidecar that you let my father borrow

Left me in abject terror. I did not think one should move so fast so close to the ground.

My sister wanted to ride again.

I was told that you were shy. I thought that you didn't like children or people in general.

And somehow you kept ending up surrounded by a tribe.

I remember you at the Quaker meetings,

Sitting in silence with your mind whirring.

Overpopulation, war, pollution, nuclear power, big business...

"David Tier got arrested protesting again," I remember people saying.

I imagined you handcuffed, tear-gassed, behind barbed wire.

But everyone around me seemed to think it was no big deal.

By the time I was in high school, I knew you as the grouchy-generous man who

Took in the outcasts, mentored the misfits.

Your hands fed strays, the animal and the human alike.

The heated monologues about the perils of the world

Were at odds with the joyful bouncing of your feet at contra dances.

We all remember you eating a pint of Ben and Jerrys and

Spotting you on a bike all over the Champlain Valley on the same day.

As my old car struggled up the Ripton Gap on the way to Boston, I would come around a corner

To find you on your bicycle, steadily climbing like the Tour de France.

And then you became "Mr. Dave" of "Grandma Donna and Mr. Dave, Tandem Bike Racing Duo."

I still do not understand your patience as you pulled her up and down all over the Vermont hills.

Boat motors appeared in the shed at mom's house, *National Geographic* in the bookshelves,

Wooden toys and new bicycles under the Christmas tree.

The magnificent Studebaker and Pogo the Boat joined the family, too.

Your hands came to hold my daughters. You shepherded them on adventures outside.

My own little girls remember you helping with training wheels, brakes, and tires.

When I saw you this summer, I still didn't wave.

I just pointed you out to my friend. "There is Mr. Dave, on his bike. He's kind of my stepfather."

I had no idea what to say when I sat down next to you on the front porch and watched the sky.

I have gotten so used to you just being here

That I come around the corner at the hardware store 900 miles away

And I see hippie's hair graying under a bright stocking cap with a winter beard and glasses,

The barrel chest atop the athlete's legs and

I always think it might be you.

Hello and goodbye, Mr. Dave.

Impatience

Maybe soon I will have a turn on mother's lap and on father's shoulders,

    And touch love and touch the sky.

Maybe soon I will be tall enough to reach the clown's stick and ride the spinning rides,

    And touch thrilling and touch joy.

Maybe soon I will be beautiful, be a woman,

    And touch the attention of the world.

Maybe soon I will get that first real kiss, that first love.

    And touch desire and touch feeling desired.

Maybe soon I will graduate,

    And touch freedom and touch adulthood.

Maybe soon I will have made the dark walk to my car, alone with keys out and senses tuned,

    And touch safety.

Maybe soon I will be settled, married, with a house and little family,

    And touch contentment and touch completeness.

Maybe soon I will start sleeping through the night,

    And touch clarity and touch sanity.

Maybe soon I will have grown children, and I will make my husband learn how to love me,

    And touch connection and touch security.

Maybe soon I will find a way to leave him,

    And touch courage and touch self-respect.

Maybe soon I will find real love,

    And touch partnership and touch home.

Maybe soon I will stop hurting,

      And touch healing and touch happiness.

Maybe soon I will feel whole,

      And touch the comfort of my own skin embracing me.

In an endless wait, always racing against death, I am impatient with hope.

My Bogeyman

My bogeyman hides in plain sight.

Familiar Lucifer lives in the ordinary, everyday rhythm of life

And comes out in the dark, when my eyes are closed,

Before I sleep, if I sleep,

Coming to hurt us.

My bogeyman sounds like the gas stove, the toaster oven, the microwave,

And burns down the house

While I sleep, if I sleep.

My children burn, burn in the flames

Fanned by that devil

Who takes the form of a kitchen towel

Soaked in the vegetable oil that someone spilled and tried to clean.

My bogeyman is invisible and

Causes dishes to slip and break on the tile floor

Leaving the clear glass

To cut our feet when we come out for a glass of water and

Leaves us bleeding silently on the kitchen floor

In the middle of the night.

My bogeyman comes through the phone

Through SnatchChat and Kick.

He/she/it reaches out and strangles my children with their own hands

While I sleep, if I sleep.

My bogeyman

Makes the dog pace outside my bedroom door,

Makes my daughters pace outside my bedroom door.

He is silent, I can only hear that he is there

In the groans of worried floorboards.

I wake,

Having failed to hear him soon enough so many other times.

I lie awake,

Ready to fight

At the slightest noise.

Becoming Tornado-Proof

I can smell trouble brewing in the air

The wind has shifted and clouds are forming.

Pulsing loathing and hopelessness surge,

Electrifying the air with emotion.

Guilt seeps through tiny spaces at the bottoms of the windows

As the house shudders.

The front door blows open,

Yielding the way doors do.

She does not try to close it behind her.

My teacup-warmed hands slip to the seat of the kitchen chair.

Disturbed, even the tag on the teabag shivers.

Its wisdom lost on that wind.

I learned early to

Batten down the hatches,

Plywood up the windows,

Encase myself in storm-cellar cement,

Watch the warnings and strain to hear the all-clear

From my cramped bunker hiding place,

The warm teacup and my half-finished poems abandoned by the overturned kitchen chair.

What if the thunder rolling no longer scared me?

Not every storm is a disaster, after all.

What if I could come out of hiding

And stand on the ground,

Sending roots in the earth and stretching myself to the sky?

Trees have structural integrity.

Or I could cultivate a second skin

With nerve endings, blood vessels, sweat glands, and hair.

Yes, I could augment my integumentary system so I can maintain emotional homeostasis.

People have been telling me to toughen up the skin I have for as long as I can remember.

Or what if I could be the microwave-proof, dishwasher-safe cup

That holds the hot mess and the icy fear served to me by others,

But only so much of it, the rest dribbling out onto the floor,

The heat warming but never melting it,

The cold cooling but never shattering it,

With a green-blue glaze shining true.

However it happens, I today will finish my tea and write my poems,

Tornado-proof.

A Walk to the Mailbox

A walk to the mailbox
Brings a stiff lemon-yellow envelope
Not addressed to me.

I know the handwriting intimately.
I can predict the angle of the slant of each letter before my eyes
Have had a chance to look away.
My heart guesses the intent of the contents before I can stop it.
Dutifully, I deliver it inside, this arrow, this invader from the past.
I deliver it inside our home where I do not want it to belong.
But it is not addressed to me.

Left on the table
Lying under the framed drawing saying
"This family runs on love"
It sits torn open.
Neither accepted nor rejected,
I can smell the decayed citrus of guilt
Leaking from the envelope.

I hear a conversation from an open bedroom door

"Would you be sad if he died, our father?"

I close the door before I can hear the messages he sent to them

Being read aloud again.

Now the envelope is hot-pink for Valentine's day.

It is girl-candy for his little girls, bait.

Does he know that they have grown into women

Who are learning to speak their minds?

He said he loved them, but it didn't feel like love to me.

A claim is staked,

A trap laid, beware of false steps.

I slip into the past and I hear his voice edge into a sneer.

"Whoops! There you go again! This is all your fault.

Look what you have done

To my family!

My family is my right, mine!

I have a right to make them love me.

To collect an obligated kiss as I walk in the door.

Give me what is mine…"

But it isn't love

Just because he insists it is.

It doesn't feel like love,

Just because he insists it is.

His special little girls look lovely in photographs.

I do not know if he still hangs the school portraits on the wall.

His lovely little girls long to be accepted, to belong,

And to have a place in the world.

They long to grow and to be happy and to love.

I am just glad that the envelopes are

No longer addressed

To me.

Validated Parking

(*Rap*)

I get to have this parking space

Paid my money for this place

Bitch, I'ma take this parking space!

See that look on yo ugly face

Validate me! Validate me!

You gotta substantiate me

I'll make you want me, Look at me!

Can you see me? Look at me!

Click! Take a picture, make a meme

Give me some more self-esteem

Look at Me look at Me look at Me look at Me Look at Me look at Me look at Me!

Hashtag validate me, yeah

Validate me! Validate me!

You gotta authenticate me

Mirror, mirror, on the door

Tell me I'm finer than that whore

Eat nothing but a salad

Scale, show me who's most valid

Validate me! validate me!

You gotta resuscitate me!

Princess need a prince, understood

Find me, wake me, kiss me good

I can be bad, I can be good,

I'll be anything I should

Validate me! Validate me!

You gotta reanimate me!

Yeah I'ma let you fill my space

know ya wanna touch that place

Man, Sing me another ballad

Man, tell me that I'm valid

Yeah, baptize, prioritize, yeah, authorize n recognize, legalize, and subsidize, legitimize my velvet thighs

I can be yo fucking soulmate

Put it up on Instagram

I'll be the one they love to hate

That's a big diamond, god damn!

Validate me! Validate me!

You gotta unliberate me

I'ma be yo baby mama,

Course our kids can go to Yale

They don't even hafta wanna

Martyr mom won't let em fail

Validate me! Validate me!

You gotta remediate me!

Max my credit to the hilt

Cost too high for you to jilt

Ain't got no shame, ain't got no guilt

'Cause I hide it like a Vanderbilt

Validate me! Validate me!

You have gotta compensate me!

Paradise is a parking lot?

I coulda bought this parking lot

I could own this whole damn spot

Now a lot of nothing's all I got, Hell!

Validate me! Validate me!

You have gotta vindicate me!

"Will you take me as I am..mmm," sing it, Joni,

"Strung out on another man"

Carolina, coming home

"Will you, will you take me as I am"

Mmm, vvvalidated parking?

Go validate yourself, girl!

Queen of Sorrows

She did not intend to rule THIS kingdom,

The village girl, muscled-strong from work,

Smart as a whip, with the sparks of mischief in her eyes.

She met the world with an irrepressible yes!

A cow sold for a little sister is a good bargain.

Yes, I will love this man!

Ends will be met, he is a good provider.

Yes, I will raise these children, and this one, too!

God doesn't give you more than you can bear.

A tidy house with a tidy yard is

Filled with rambunctious sons.

Such a good-looking family!

And so smart and so proud in the clothes she saved up to buy for them.

It was not supposed to be like this.

The funerals. Family reunion at the graveyard.

The double vision, looking through the present to see what once was.

Buying groceries for the dead.

And beds and chairs for the ghosts.

Like a dragon, she carefully guards her treasures as they slowly decay.

Yesterday's takeout is hidden behind the one from last year.

The weight, oh the weighty heaviness threatens to drown her in bitterness.

She deserved so much more.

Holding court

With a scepter of self-righteousness and

The power of pity.

Take this crown! She almost pleads.

No! She must never forget.

The craft from long-ago Sunday school

Is gifted with sorrow.

How is it that the queen is locked in her own tower

Counting martyr gold?

Her fist closes tight around this currency of grief.

God does not give you more than you can bear,

      Except when He does.

Vision

A flash creates a curve in the straight edge,

Yielding bends in the harsh infinity of parallel lines.

Tissue paper dampened with mucus and tears begins

To thin, to thin, and then

Disintegrates into pools of color.

Blurs, softness, fuzzy auras spread the light with a wet brush

Bleeding out over the hard edges of the darkness.

There is beauty there in the haze, the uncertainty, the diffuse pattern of light.

The missing patches fill themselves in, unbidden.

Is it not all just speculation taken on faith?

The mind is an unruly thing craving barred cages of order over joyous chaos.

Which human gods can truly see around corners?

The universe constantly remakes itself.

Explosions from the darkness punch black holes with giant fists

Leaving lightless voids behind the myths and constellations.

Light consumed

Light deflected

Light refracted

Light reflected

Light redacted

Light magnified

No matter the origin and no matter the path,

No matter the blindness of impending night,

I choose to look away from the growing shadow

And stare in awe at the quality of the light.

Pictures of My Grandfather

Last night I realized that I have no real pictures of Grandfather.

He was there at my wedding, but he managed to escape all cameras.

Wait; is that his arm near Grandmother? And I think that may be him carrying that bucket of flowers, and adjusting the table just so.

Mostly all I have of him are the pictures in my mind:

A suitcase full of vitamins

Adding machine tape curling ever longer as the cigarette ash threatened to fall with each clack

Clothes steamer hissing in the backroom

The lovingly worn soft leather seats of the purple Volvo as he drove

"Have some more, it'll put hair on your chest!" Said with a wry smile as I thought, horrified, that I did not want hair on my little girl chest.

The Humphrey Bogart look that my father, who looks so much like him, never had the charisma to pull off

The details man, the finish man sanding and varnishing, sanding and varnishing, sanding and vanishing…

The sudden smile in the unexpected place and a short bark of laughter, the sharp comment bringing things back down to earth

The other end of the table while Grandmother was holding court in a house full of cousins

The love of Beauty, not bothering to wax poetic (he was actually waxing)

Noticing the flaws, working, scheming, dreaming, risking, moving, working

He was not caught in the pictures, now I remember, because he was too busy holding up his corner of the world, showing us how it is done.

Things that Spin

The winds of doubt sweep in,

Knock helicopter seeds away from their tie-downs in high branches.

Drawn into the spiral

Spinning, twirling, whirling,

Whirligig thought-seeds

Swirl like dirty mop-water down the drain.

Maple, ash, sycamore shed samaras.

Only a few will unfurl to

Land and plant new life.

The Silent Ones

The silent ones are revealed in the morning fog

By a flick of tail.

So close they stand, with

Legs like sapling trunks, lit

By the fingered pattern of light filtered through poplar leaves.

Heads lift from grazing, tilting in unison.

We are all frozen

In that endlessly suspended instant

Until the crack of an acorn dropping to the ground to

Break the spell.

Uninvited

The night came at noon,

An uninvited guest staying long past the point of welcome.

Her suitcases overflow with cold drizzle-rain.

The wet seeps into the tips of my fingers to steal the warmth that should live there.

Hot bath, hot coffee, spicy food, ten minutes on the exercise machine, but still

The chill clings to the space beneath my skin and will not be evicted as

The smell of grayness pushes deeper, seeking my innermost rooms.

The false night speaks in the staccato of sleet.

"Tick, tick," she names the clock a liar

Until I give in and take her gray with me under blankets.

Today there will be no poetry.

Held in the Lap of These Mountains

I could never be at home by the sea,

Sea of water,

Sea of grass,

Sea of sand,

My voice swallowed by the great expanse,

Hurricane vulnerable,

Storm-tossed with

No protection from sun and wind,

Susceptible

To being washed away by fickle moon-tides.

There is safety in the lap of these mountains.

I drove the winding roads

Clinging to her side,

Following the Appalachians south.

I fled for miles upon miles

But I never left her lap.

In the mountains, I am small, inconsequential.

My failures and successes mean nothing

And still, I am lovingly held, accepted.

She loves all of her grandchildren the same.

Layers etched against the sky,

The horizon itself is curved by the rise of her hips and shoulders.

The warm shawl of colors, soft-wrinkled with age and

Handwoven on an ancient loom,

Changes hues with the cycle of seasons as it

Flows along her curves.

Her royalty is understood, no need to wear a crown.

Even in darkness, I feel her generous embrace,

Calm, constant, comforting, never too tight.

The mountains do not need me to be

Anything,

Anywhere,

Anyone,

Someone.

The mountains just are.

Sunday Morning Walks

I have seen the cathedrals of France,

Felt the vibrations of pipe organs,

Heard the call from the minarets rising above dusty streets.

I have chanted in Sanskrit on an incense-soaked ashram,

Drank decaffeinated coffee from Unitarian urns,

Sat in twitchy silence in the meeting house,

And tasted apples dripping with honey for a sweet new year.

Yet, I am ever called to Sunday morning walks.

The trees are my congregation, bowing and waving in the wind, each one a unique character.

The smell of the river, ripe with mud and wet roots, replenishes my spirit.

The light filtered through the leaves and vines is my divine story in stained glass.

My hymn is the rhythm of my own feet as my legs flow freely from my hips at their own natural pace.

May peace be with you,

And also with me.

One Woman's Trash

Learn to love the broken:

The cup with a chip,

The bowl with the hairline crack only visible from the inside.

But I need to be needed,

To mend, to fix, to clean, to rehome and

To feel better than those chipped cups in my cabinet,

      The unmatched sock in my drawer,

      The old silver spoon with the spot of tarnish.

      The chair with the pattern like an alien face, scarred by the cat's claw.

But I need only a few things, why hang on to the damaged,

      The clutter,

      The mess?

But my new life is for nice new things,

      For a nice new me.

When did cleaning up, cleaning out, moving on, become hiding pieces of me from myself?

I feel like an antique, something old and worn hoping to be cherished for its story.

Should I like only the shiny pieces of myself that smell like a newly opened plastic bag?

How do I learn to love the broken without drowning in brokenness,

Wondering as I sip from a chipped cup, lovingly, one last time.

Forest and Tree

for Debra

Strong   and   Flexible,   Rooted   and   Sky-reaching,

Designed by nature   To shelter and to survive,

Your branches   Bend and flex

With the accustomed weight.

But wait,

You are

Not a tree,

But a human

In the great forest

Of humanity.

Your joy is contagious

Like your courage.

Laugh in that way that you do,

With the sparkle of mischief

Soaked in the wisdom of pain.

Sway in a dance just for you

And let someone else hold up the sky

For a moment...   Or maybe two.

For Julia on the Occasion of Her Birthday
(*We won't say which one*)

"Tell me some good news,"
She hails from her comfortable shoes

As we watch sunsets over bookshelves
On Wednesday and Thursday nights.

She always keeps busy
Keeping up with everyone.

Trampoline Juju tosses blonde hair with her grandbaby,
The mischief of the two-year-old in her smile.

She takes great pleasure
In the work of being exactly who she is.

A Second Coming or She Comes Again, Not a Porno Story

So this is coming of age, mid-life style.

Just like before, I feel the late bloomer but my body disagrees.

I remember 12 and 22, those bookends of the "coming of age time."

A YA novel: kill off the parents or make them super busy somehow to get them out of the way.

> Now the plot can begin where our heroes solve a few problems by themselves and run into the brick wall of the world, ouch!

> Find a little love interest and some big strength and walk with bruises and scrapes into the sunrise of "real life."

Yep, been there, done that!

> And read the book and saw the movie, and aced a course in YA lit at grad school.

For a time, I felt like a grown-up. I was smarty-wise, absolutely certain that I knew my assigned place.

> I told myself that this was as good as it gets, no more change needed. I accepted my fate.

> Who am I? White-mother-daughter-wife-librarian-teacher-vegetarian-smalltown-good citizen. Next question?

Now when my inner voice screams, "Who am I?"

> I sass back "The garbage truck, that's who!"

> Wait, no, that's not me...I read that somewhere in a children's book.

I remember hitting twitchy, prickle-itchy, puberty and doing the math.

> "I am going to be 31 in the year 2000. Gasp! That is so old! I'll be middle-aged and settled in for the ride towards the big sunset if nuclear war doesn't get us first."

Butterflies are beautiful, but I am not a butterfly,

> Maybe Dr. Frankenstein tried to make a butterfly while posting it on YouTube.

> My transformation is messy and public.

2020 is fast approaching and I am 50. What!?!

I feel anything but settled, just as twitchy, prickle-itchy in my skin now that puberty has left the building. What is this body I am in? It mostly works but feels teenage-mutant foreign.

Yes, I am still a mother in the middle of mothering

And a daughter in the middle of daughtering

And I am busy wifing, too.

In the midst of life

I'm in a play, off, off, off-broadway, and

I do not know how long my run will be.

These days it is more like an improv sketch.

I no longer believe in fate, only biological inevitability.

I just want to accept myself. And have a good laugh with her.

Rebirth

The deep hurdy-gurdy chorus of cicadas

Pierces the weight of liquid air,

Passing through the window glass and

Shouting down the air conditioner.

The air thrums with the ease of summer evenings.

With a shiver of sunburned arms the dark begins to fall.

The thrum is eclipsed by the higher bark of cricket and katydids

When the moon takes over the sky.

I didn't even realize how much I had missed them

And their vibrations of rebirth.

Dear Me at age 21,

You are stronger than you know, tougher than you have ever suspected. You will be just fine.

You know how to love, so just work on loving yourself. There is no need to try to impress other people. You are loved already and you will be loved in the future, but maybe not by the people you expect. Your awkwardness is cool. You are brave. Your brain is prone to be misguided by fear, so remember to check in with your gut. Trust your gut, it is pretty good.

You are truly beautiful and you will become more beautiful with age. Don't worry so much about picking up other people's messes. You can't actually fix people. People will not love you more or keep you safe because of what you have done for them. Work on your own messes! Be who you are and invite others in when YOU want to. You will also have to uninvite some people and listen when others uninvite you.

It is okay to fail. It is okay to succeed. It is okay to feel the happiness and excitement. It is okay to feel the pain and disappointment. It is okay to feel ashamed and embarrassed. Be as honest with yourself as you can. It is okay to love yourself just as you are. You will still grow and change. There will always be more to discover and you are curious by nature. You will always value connection. You do have social skills, no matter what anyone says. You will never know it all. You will never have much control over the world because no one does, but you can still love the world. You still have so much to learn and experience. Enjoy!

Take care,

Kyra, age 50 and a half

About the author

Kyra Freeman writes poems, tells stories, and dances in the kitchen in Morganton, North Carolina. A former school librarian turned massage therapist; she was raised in Vermont not too far from the Appalachians. She lives with her family and infamous pets and goes outside in the yard as much as possible.

Salad

Today I am eating salad with a spoon.

Who packed this lunch, anyway?

"She did," my reflection quips at me from the back of the spoon.

Spoonfuls of lettuce shed an almond on the way to my mouth,

Leftover chicken from on top is sliced away in chunks and bits with metal edge of the spoon,

A spot of escaped dressing rests on my lap.

It is delicious.

www.ingramcontent.com/pod-product-compliance
Lightning Source LLC
Chambersburg PA
CBHW081157090426
42736CB00017B/3361

9781952485244